BREATH TAKES

BREATH TAKES

Douglas Barbour

Wolsak and Wynn . Toronto

Typeset in Times New Roman, printed in Canada by The Coach House Printing Company, Toronto.

Cover art: © Robert Sinclair – *Moondance*, 1995
Cover design: Coach House
Author's photograph by Bill Beard

Breath Ghazals #s 1, 2, 4, 5, 7, 8, 11, & 12 appeared in *Visible Visions: Selected Poems* (NeWest Press 1984).

The author is grateful to the editors of the following journals, in which versions of many of these poems first appeared: *Antigonish Review, Essays on Canadian Writing, Descant, The Fiddlehead, filling station, Grain, Malahat Review, Mattoid* (Australia), *Nimrod: International Journal of Poetry and Prose (O! Canada), Prairie Fire, Rubicon, Sulfur* (USA), *Tinfish* (Hawai'i). Also to *Catalyst* (Perth, Australia and Cambridge, England: SALT Publishing, forthcoming), edited by John Kinsella.

The publishers gratefully acknowledge the support of the Canada Council for the Arts and the Ontario Arts Council.

The Canada Council | Le Conseil des Arts
for the Arts | du Canada

ONTARIO ARTS COUNCIL
CONSEIL DES ARTS DE L'ONTARIO

Wolsak and Wynn Publishers Ltd
192 Spadina Avenue, Suite 315
Toronto, ON
Canada M5T 2C2

National Library of Canada Cataloguing in Publication Data

Barbour, Douglas, 1940-
    Breath takes

Poems.
ISBN 0-919897-78-9

I. Title.

PS8553.A76B74 2001   C811'.54   C2001-902390-1
PR9199.3.B37B74 2001

For Sharon

& friends everywhere

I chose poetry because every line set out
so hopefully from a new margin, and
because my heart was hot and unbowed.

Michele Leggott

CONTENTS

Breath Ghazals

& The Returns

Notes   77

BREATH GHAZALS

so that the day remains open
the next collision in the light
and catch up to the breath
breathing somewhere

                     the air

as it comes out ahead of me

                             Fred Wah

breath ghazal 1:

poised on the knife edge between this line & the next
the pulse in the base of my thumb   thumping

something spills across the page
if you hear me   do you hear me bleed

now that sound   hah   huh
if you pay attention   you owe at ease

so we pass thru   that barrier too
from opposite ends of the table   eat

i wanted that   now i want this
no   you   i mean   listen

breath ghazal 2:

among the many leaves
surround me   listen

phtt   phtt phtt
tlip   tlip   tlip   so

softly & apart   look
only grey clouds slightly

cross the sun   phtt
tlip   you   listen

rain drums   soft
on leaves   spaced apart

breath ghazal 3:

dusk valleys   dark   sky
s a/light   page   turning

with what signs written darkly across
ridges   runes carved of   space

signification   how to read
this alphabet of built & grown world tangled

stark presence   perhaps   breath (uhh) taking
sky utter light   slowly darkens   clear

the messages change too fast breath
less to say   to see thems   enough

breath ghazal 4:

Inbreathing   she said   take out
aaaah   a moments temptation taking in

ward off   what rose white   a light
overflowing the dark   surrounding

that instant   & that breath   so
still   years later   held now

like withholding comprehension   or some
thing   like that   holding back

nothing   let it go   now   out
breathing too saaaa   heh   (yeh)

breath ghazal 5:

tell me when youre going under
he said .   im going under   im

going uh   thats how fast
it was .   it is   an

aesthetic response   almost   distanced
the breathing smooth   calm   controlled

now its over   the pain you might have felt
gone   youre tired   yr eyes close

listen to the quiet way   you   in
hale   exhale   efff   fff   efff   fff

breath ghazal 6:

moving thru   & listening for
birdsong crisscrossing treetops

wind rushing roadside grasses
sudden flap of wings behind a bush

i also hear   ah hah ahh   haahh
these other sounds   counterpoint

pump of heart   lungs
muscle shifts   meat

groaning   in slow celebration
of its bloody life   moving thru

breath ghazal 7:

seabreath   it open smooth   it
odour move   it wave

smash chest   smack sand
whoooshaahh it go out   again

sound is here   breath   look
sniff it   wash of salt tang fish

smell   it flare nostrils   open ears
to susurration on sand   those particles

the worlds slow breathing   breaking
moon heaving   it   in   &   out

breath ghazal 8:

Fuck off fuck off fuck off
i cant breathe   when you stand too close

id never kill myself for you
for you arent worth the least sacrifice

for you   i might piss out an open window
on a dark muggy evening   holding my breath

as if you   were with me again
again   youre trying too hard to make it seem real

go on   the doors over there   yeah
close it behind you   aah   haahh

breath ghazal 9:

life homelessness to will
because enter sorrow

breathe far   of has escape
the your cannot you not because

cannot you have the mineral
you welcome all the portholes

separate green   cannot an to
because formless   the breathe because

breathe you the your
breathe

breath ghazal 10:

'easeful death' is nothing so easy
as said   that easy breath easing out

to where   in the cool disappearing air
a soft cloth covers the eyes   the mouth

the head against a pillow   resting it seems
still   where the well wrapt body lies

lies   lies   the eyes seem to be trying
to say   slowly   fading   soon to close

forever on a sigh   last exhalation   feather
unmoved   the mirror mist fading   aaah   gone

breath ghazal 11:

ok spring   ive got you figured   this time
returning   breath for breath

you inhale   slow inebriation
breathe out the growth   waaa—idening green

every shade of   intoxication   non toxic
photosynthesis   filling the trees & grass

buds swell   they fill with fresh air
inhaled   sunlight   & they are   a light

for a few days only   you can almost hear them
brightly breathing in the sharp spring air

breath ghazal 12:

smell the body sniff the skin
under the sheets the slight aroma magnifies

along magnetic lines of inner power
manifest in rising   filling flesh

follow yr nose yr tongue lightly moving
across expanses of clean salty beaches   hf hf

it grows with desire   glows with it
look   yr face my face   nuzzle in armpit   groin

this all smells so good   'O taste and
see'   loves signal odour mists the air

breath ghazal 13:

jagged
leavetakings

Fall
sing

i loved you
you knew

slow fade
winter breath

exhalation
below zero

breath ghazal 14:

heavy breathing   leading you on
beyond   what boundary

the openings of flesh   the hills
you climb to see   the other side

what calls   from love to love
that landscape   not yet seen

aaah   the intake of breath at the vision
green/blue   there is that world you wish

to enter   run towards
even beyond yr heart   heavy/   heaa (breathing

breath ghazal 15:

desire eats the breath away   inside ?
desire   desires that breath & all else   stay

there   holding yr breath   you stand
as one   two held in a breath of discovery

but whats discovered between the intake
& the outrush   the slow unfolding of air

in her hair   caresses the finest down on her neck
her breath slows as it enters you   you

know desire   it eats away at everything
outside   fire in the lungs   it wont subside

breath ghazal 16:

no
you say

go .
ok   ok   im

going   im going   but
its not that easy

taking it in
halation of what my heart refuses

to know   a sighhh   the loss
of breath on the wind of my goodbye

18

breath ghazal 17:

for Roger Zelazny

hard for a breath i tarry   harried
into the body of time   no   please

yet the lack of breath
s death   even in movement the care

taking the earth & its air   making
the ruined lands fair   again

not for the clanking machines waiting
so long for the breathing monstrosities under

standing reason from beyond it   in love
desire   in breathing (& out)   to say that   Now

breath ghazal 18:

what i can trust is simple   perhaps
effff   simply not what i sense

surrounds us .   oh i believe it   yet
our great fear is that there

s nothing more than *signs*   there
we read with those senses   we dont

quite trust .   yet do i really   not
believe .   i do not .   i simply breathe

aaah   hahh   & something in me trusts then
the air   does surround us   moving thru

19

breath ghazal 19:

'Failure, ultimately, under erasure.'
Smaro Kamboureli

take a deep breath   blow
the tracings of the word in rubber   off

the paper   clean again   *rubbed*
clean   to begin again   fool / write

i wanted to *say*   something my
mistake   to try to write it down

something of pain   something of
joy   physical   it startled thru my body

& i wrote it down   watched it disappear
& so erased it   then blew it all away   *whoof*

breath ghazal 20:

its a long story   (take yr time)   tell
tale delights   delicious   de

lays it on the line   of a new thought
desire propels   but how far   aaahh

room for lots of telling details
traces of desired body to read

& listen for   *your* speech   aah   the story
unraveling   tongues in our mouths sighs

breath on our faces   ('lovers'   signs
a kind of closure   pleasure binds

breath ghazal 21:

i cd tell you of pain   but pain
fully i know i dont know what this pain is .

or if it is .   if it is pain
its almost pain less the usual daily strain

of taking the air .   in .   efff .
in pain   you might say .   breathing .

i breathe   & drink & eat .   & i dont
know whats happening .   its that abstract .

its that real .   i wd tell you of that pain
but i dont know what im talking about .   again .

breath ghazal 22:

mis take   mis
taken   i dent   i ty

myself up in knotted argument
broken scenes   flow gone awry

broken by   stifled awareness of
feeling breaking against what

barriers of perception   they
get in the way   get away

from there   its dangerous   you
cant breathe   (huhaaa   (ohh   you do

breath ghazal 23:

the air lies heavy on the lake   waves still
is it before or after   the storm

the air we breathe   eefff   heavy
with our bodies sweat heavy

odour of love lies with us still   after
or before we move   a gentle ex

halation   fffaa   halo of lamplight
in your hair   in the dusk

huge drops kiss the lake
drum lightly on the roof above our heads

breath ghazal 24:

trace the outlines of your face
fluffed hair   in the air   of an evening gone

without trace .   imaginations only .   i think
therefore i was there .   imaginations only

reality made fiction .   memory is fitful   only
the air we breathe   what we know for sure

is there .   any way   i breathed
your breath in that shimmering darkness   you

breathed mine .   aahh   imagination insists
all traces are real .   the air full   of our losses .

breath ghazal 25:

Aaagh   that isnt
what i meant to say   he says

Ooooh   thats what
you always say   she says

their breathing steady   still   un
steady they wait for the other to speak

sniff the odour of their anger to
gether   denying togetherness

eeugh   i can almost taste it
all that held in speech   explode in a sigh

breath ghazal 26:
                    for Chet Baker

inhale   almost unnoticed   then
blow breathy notes as the melody soars

blue notes bent with the breath
of an asthmatic dying fall

he insists hes been there   no   listen
hard to breathe till the shit hits home

years enough of that lost song   till re
habilitation   got him

brought him   back   those
gorgeous soft big notes so gently breathed

breath ghazal 27:

epithalamium for Wendy & Bill

the room is full of flowers   take
a deep breath   hhfff   say i do

outside   the play of rain
s another sign for your marriage

if you want them they surround you   you
want only to say   love

it is to take that step
breathing the heady air of the room

smile at each other   breathe   yourselves
step out   beyond both flowers or rain

breath ghazal 28:

i can step with this poem out of time
i think .   a lyric lying lightly on my tongue

but breathe   'out of thought eternity: Cold
Pastoral'   in the dead of winter   white traces

hang scattered in air   vistas fade   fantastic
cityscapes of the human intention to speak to

what   is the inhalation   for
but to push it all out   after   fffaaahhh

further   to this deponent says   nothing
a silence so loud it can be read across the sky

breath ghazal 29:

angelology makes snow angels new   now
where in the ancient hierarchy can i find them

theories abound   as always   but i
want to know   how explain this presence of absence

hole in the snow   an emptiness shining
imprint of glory   if youre lucky   no footprints

now i begin to comprehend   fear of angels
how wrestle intaglios   those empty spaces

they are there   only as they are not there
they are bright & white &   never breathe   not once

breath ghazal 30:

outside the window   darkness & white snow below
in it my eyes in my face   reflect   curious

i stare at the eyes which stare back
& in them   thru them   see light reflecting snow

hollowed out of the dark   mirror on the wall
at my back   reflects all   night   & transparent me

i lean closer   look down   to bright white ground
the glass bears my breath   light traces filigree out

while i peer &   breathe intent   frost thickens & grows
in the mirror behind me   only a white window shows

breath ghazal 31:

i want to whisper magic in yr ear   all
ways   a small sigh will do it   aahhh

the wordless *tells*   as small cries
intensify   momentum moving to that space   hidden

in the body of time   eyes closed   the air of
the others lungs enters yr own   a quiet breeze

a story told over & over   it is so simple   &
it refuses   to enter discourse   courses thru yr body

breathing easier   now   out   the story over
& over again   magic repeat   breathing in & out

breath ghazal 32:

open up   take a deep   euaghh
breathe it out   haaahh   it

say that to me   i   it   out
there   in   it   euughh in me

it comes   in   it is   all
around   it breathe   too   in

to what we say we know   we
breathe such   understanding   the smell of

the world   it say   open up
take me in   yes   effff

breath ghazal 33:

i want to hold the moment in my hands
& know its no illusion

touch the body   & say
the body language

i want to breathe the odours
of love   or   efff

lust will do   the raw
of desire   is finally just the intaken breath

at the moment you say with yr body
i / love / you

breath ghazal 34:

for E.D. Blodgett, from whom i stole the first line

'When Francis of Assisi spoke'
Orpheus turned back a moment too soon

turned back   holding his breath   tense with fear
& irruptive desire   yet seeing nothing hears   still music

fall from the air   brightening beckoning night   his
answering song Hers   Hers   forever

Francis will never comprehend   his Mother   loves
the birds   but doesnt really hear their song

they praise Her   though he deny it
with his dying breath a dying fall

breath ghazal 35:

after seeing Tarkovsky's *Stalker*

clearwater ripples over history & faith
revolutionary acts & the words of our forebears

only the harsh intake of breath   uh   uh   uh
the dreaming   man remains

remains: boneyards of the soul   skeletons
of automatics   the structure of loss   of hope   still

there were fires   earth beneath their feet
continually shifted   the flowing mirrors   &

always   always   air in the lungs   continued
vision   shifts   in mist   back   back   in time

breath ghazal 36:

at night beside this body   once again   you lie
in this world too   & in those others

where are you   in light/nightly haling the cool air
air of summer   air of ocean   air of northern mists

wearing what   wherein you move   warily
where are you   (now)   rem sleep takes you there

you move across   a glade   a beach   an island
& with whom   & do you really want to come back

night dissipates   full moon fades in light
ning sky   hear yr breaths (sigh) gather you home

breath ghazal 37:

who breathes beyond   & unto me   the world
i do not know   i do not know

a thing   the worlds a kind
of breathing   & could stop

the breathing worlds   beyond me
but im in it   & i breathe

inspired   id say   but by
or   to

who breathes beyond i do not know but feel
sometimes the rhythm   with   ah!   bright lungs!

breath ghazal 38:

speak of the breath   sighing
out of the mouth   softly

across the ear   hairs trembling
(drumbeats) in the gentle airs   of one   alive

to say   love   to say   want
to say   so gently   come

now   yes   just like that
(tympanum)   yes   oh   please   enter

what are called   the gates
of life / dreams   ahh   ahhh   aahhhh

breath ghazal 39:

its an easy fall   slipslide
all the way   into   what

ancient discourse   this core   dis
covery of 'love'   always 'as if'

breath coming 'now'   in short 'sweet' gasps
when 'you' are here   near   hear

my heartbeat answer 'your' presence
skin flush with pleasure   yeah sure   'for'

the pressure on ribcage   ooohh   hiss of breath
ssaaa 'the first time'   it happens   again

breath ghazal 40:

soft inhalation of breath efff   i
dentity   efff   i

dentify the sound   'ah me' if
only that lyric lie

of the intake   efff   in
ward   gaze of the eye

middle of the forehead
flushed over   vision turned

in upon itself   the material ego
which matters only as 'I' say   i sigh

breath ghazal 41:

imagine the possibility of a held breath   'you'
stand silent where small waves wash gentle in

then sigh   fffmm   as embers lost in grey
darken double in reflection   a shift

of attention huh   here   & there   where
night slowly gathers charcoal in

smolder   a lone star flickers /   drifts
above solid points of light along the shore

where are you   why do i try
to imagine you   standing there   breathing still

breath ghazal 42:

day dark descends   car lights
& exhaust on the grey streets

a winged shape lost in mist
metallic buzz of falling angels wings ?

depression lowering   fall   fall
the ashes on the wind   strewn

a morning continues   grey
slides over everything rendered insubstantial

now   no breath   still
the rain does not descend

breath ghazal 43:

birds soar
from roaring branches

bent before the wind which takes them high
leaves   not birds

in flight   from storm
bright against the dull grey sky

breathe   aaah   chinese calligraphy
onto the clear air   soon

falling snow   not leaves
absents the river from your questing eye

breath ghazal 44:

desiring *against* lyric   hearing
all those voices

beyond any eyes   site
of what inspired inward vision   inscribed

of just one self   on the shelf
of all those old conventions   no

listen   whoever speaks here
speaks for itself   alone   a soul

solely lost in the airwaves
breathing deeply   *eefff*   & taking them in

breath ghazal 45:

your entrance   fills my lungs
expand   air & free   i move

to embrace   — aaah   what (in)de
cision   light of the temple   cuts in(de)

scribe —   a cry of love   gentle
insistent sound   against di

vision   in the thin air of
that light pouring down   a now ex

cathedra   perception of loss in finding
a breath to hold   onto   you   here in —

breath ghazal 46:
               a partial repeat

your entrance   into me
id say   my lungs expand   air & free i

move to embrace   ooh yes   what de
liverance   light in the temple   an

open book   our feelings now   on
words   small cries of love   inhaled out

warding off other readings   of the moment
awry   lost beginning   on edge then

you came into the room   again
i didnt know you   & then i caught my breath   ahh

breath ghazal 47:

leaves   fall
in   noted beneficence

wind takes them   fresh
laden   cool in lungs   too

effff ffffmm   over &   over
transforming   hue   & you

move   too   these days
thru a maze of colours   fallen

beneath our feet
crunch yytwheesh   whioosh   where

breath ghazal 48:

the heady heavy sweetseemin' smell of new-mown grass
asserts a generation September song denies   haahh

seed broken   seed frozen   harbinger ?
that odour   effff   seems to promise birth

but spring is far behind   now   &
i breathe a colder story on the morning wind

winding down   this is the final cut
the plot fixed   ending known   an odour of decay

not quite   now green is still greener
than it will be   & the cool breath is still   aahh   sweet

breath ghazal 49:

                   'a blues'

breath   death   ai eeee
breath   death   aii eeeee

such wealth of meaning in a harsh rhyme
pump   eugh   pump   heugh

lungs / bellows / fire
the recalcitrant heart

beneath a bright night sky
stars come & go   red or blue shift

universe   take yr deep breaths too
expand & contract to the same longing song

breath ghazal 50:

                   in memoriam bpNichol

air   clouds   all
semes   gone   in

absentia   yet felt
aahhh   a sharpness in the air

inscribes   his departure
even deeper in the heart & lungs

body refuses to know this absence
phantom limb   phantom

breath   'you' hear as
his spirit ascends thru the city of clouds

breath ghazal 51:

now they say   its over
over   now   past

tense   they feel 'it' slide away   a
momentary   lapse of a

tension   they never knew they
felt   'the moment's grace'   now lost

because they always tried 'to catch it'
'i' wish theyd caught on   sooner

every breath   efff   or fffeh
is here   & now   & here & now   again

breath ghazal 52:

i could say im getting old now too   too
often i feel it   a harsh

intake of air   an ache somewhere
going nowhere hannh   ahahh

besides the air seems colder longer   now
the longer i stay to notice the way

my body no longer finds the edge
as close as a while ago   more

clothing   more food   more
of my foolish complaints   for / get it

breath ghazal 53:

for Fred Wah

to say it all   you need big lungs
that heavy intake   then a slow rush

of words   you say   you found them
gathering   twisting them together

all that miscellany   into a nest like
like that bird you spoke for   not mine

id say a loon   probably
in the distance   as the sun

appears or disappears at the horizon
gone deep   & hiding there silent holding its breath

breath ghazal 54:

(also for Fred)

or how you say   dance it
all those squiggly figures   so long

ago   on the go   going down into
the stone   inscription   & you

trip over it   inhale sharply   aach
pick yrself up holding your knee

out of the hunt   the dance   & so
copying it at a distance   sharpening

your glance   in stone   incise   in/
scape the held breath of inspiration all those long stone years

breath ghazal 55:

whats lost elsewhere   leaves
the trees blown outward   whooosha

all those colours gone into darkness
under the earth   no breath   left

of wind   or scandal   to sing   to dance
drunk in among the sly belles

of a ball   bouncing in time
you   & the others   we know

well carry on   putting leaves
back on the tree   a worlds worth

breath ghazal 56:

a:
at that precise instant watching i draw
out of synch   with them   in   aahh

across   behind   & thru   the net of winter branches
brownian movement of   waxwings

irregulars in this flypast
a precision lost in dissolution   an ordered

disorder ?   so fast &   dis
continuous   their flight   yet   the sky

between their waving lines   appeared
a kind of pattern   almost   in the blink of an eye

b:
how at that precise instant indrawn
out of synch   with them   aahhh

allatonce across behind & thru the net of winter branches
brownian movement of wings & bodies

write that   wave \|/\|/ sine   how
many   numbers weave   never known

for sure   the waxwings there   a flow
wings stuttering so fast they touch

neither branches nor each other
winging suddenly absent in a sweep of gesture of

banners in the wind   'flif flif'
whos holding breath silent watching them disappear

breath ghazal 57:

youthful adoration brings life again
here there is more than memory can bear

mouth to mouth re /   citation
burrowing in to where bodies rime

exquisite   odour of love open
sing   ardour   arbour

beneath that famous tree
the wine   the bread   the vow

love is breathing deeply   letting
go   aahh   oohhh   yes   do

breath ghazal 58:

somehow 'i' was lost   in the exhaust
of crowded cars   heading to what

destination   delusion   de nature
of which when stopped dead in a lineup

s of no consequence to the coughing mind
breathing carbon monoxide   heh hah

breathing breakdown   heugh   a mist of fumes
hides the world from sight   folded hills

greens   rolling away   breakers roaring white
against once-empty beaches now tracked to industrial time

breath ghazal 59:

(Barrier Reef Snorkeling)

breathe easy   breathe even   &
even as your breath is taken

away   they go   striped   bright
multicoloured swimmers in

this muted dream of ocean alive   aahh
haahh   even through the mouth to

disconnected air above   eyes below
open to a world   of living   crystalline

branches of the mothering tree of life
growing always infinitesimally   toward the light

breath ghazal 60:

Ahm   sim
plicity

or   com   ah   that
metropolis of mind

youre likely to get lost in
no   'i' am

ouch   even a sigh
slips nets of single syllables gone wrong

'i' should be singing a simple song
less signed against than signing   all along

breath ghazal 61:

phphphh   phphh   the living touch
of breath breathed upon you

thats gesture   thats this moment
every moment   potential

this is deliberate   this is
an exercise of the lungs as the heart venturing

into the air   there touched *into*
life   that chaos   that impressions

known only   even to be sorted   efff
efff   as i live and breathe   fffe

breath ghazal 62:
>   for Joe Henderson

continuing intake for the gesture
outward of a melody

'written on the wind'   that song   'as
if'   in an almost human voice

eefff   you take it in   all
to let it flow out & over notes smeared together soaring

in harsh beauty   spiraling cries
which ever way you choose

across the given   & beyond it
giving back breath sounding the made new

Hawkesbury River Sequence
3 for Robert Adamson

breath ghazal 63:

breathing a fresh fishy marrow of day leaving
the reaches of light & water   standing

on the wooden dock   Junos indrawn breath & click
of camera catching the last measure of shadow

on face & far shore   Aaahh   that does it   Dark
always falling through darkness somewhere

breathing   to talk   that translation
of breath   efff   into words world connecting

just above the water line   a kind of pause of light
reflecting darkly the shapes of people inhaling communion
                                                                        above it all

breath ghazal 64:

in the darkening air above the rivers gentle lapping
a tapping of water against the thicker atoms of grey wood

Mercury hovers   at least in speech
just beyond reach his silver winged sandals

catch the last rays of sun .   turn gold
hes not himself easily caught   mutable / unstable

& the rising balloon of alchemical speculation
remains always below him   now

beyond the inturning *heoough* of philosophy
gentle laughter of friends inhaling the air of his passing

breath ghazal 65:

'The afternoon's last light has gone under now'   & if
'a flying fox swims in through a star'   reflected

if only in your words breathed
across the windows warm light

before in shadowing air   or behind
in the warmth itself

the soft *aaahh* of awe   of all
language still allows

even with the fax chittering into flame
these words fingered far beyond hope   beyond all nets

breath ghazal 66:
                              in memoriam John Thompson/1995

When he was alive   a large man
outdoors   he took big breaths   aaahh   into

the poems   even their silences
breathed   (fffmn)   those dark gaps

he grew too used to   to fall in
to   the darkness   welcomed

in words still full of the in
halation   but what went out   in silence

there   was great love   still   breathing
& an intense hatred   growing   all out of breath

44

Hawkesbury River Sequence continued

Two more for Robert Adamson: 09 VI 95.

breath ghazal 67:

mornings as if the whole place held its breath
the open mouth of the reach   at

tention   silence & sun are laid upon
it   a lightness of awe

move in that green silence down
toward the mirroring water   the bright

mudflats glowing beneath bright blue
& green   then breathe a heady mixture

of fresh air bush & ocean almost
the world inhales again   aaahh

breath ghazal 68:

Gathered with beer & wine in warm dusk
we sip slowly as you begin to tell the story

just beyond the outdoor tables small circle of light
in the dark air   a deeper darkness

rustling closer in the tall gums
flames crackle in your voice   carrying

us with you along the river   all lit up
night flaring then   *in* tense   telling

details the comedy of electricity for beer
as the police hauled everyone out of town

but you & your friend   with more beer
(your grin   words   subtle air of

disbelief   *in* the telling too our
breaths almost held   in listening   efff

as the wall of fire moves downriver   & you
two move your boat up toward that utter halt

through black & red banks of fired trees
guzzling beer & insisting on seeing the thing itself

wall of heat turns you back   now assured of a next time
down wind again   as you tell it   & sigh   fffmmmm

breath ghazal 69:

for a country nearly lost: 31 X 95.

Ffmmm   a sigh of relief   country
matters   or the land does   ground

of our being here   so far
& wide   so many   & the spirit of

all that   a brea[d]th of   of
inspiration   how could we take in

the whole reach of it   that distance overcome
that we would allow   in deference   difference

that we would sit together & weave
from all the separate strands a quilt to warm us   aaahh yes

breath ghazal 70:
                              and again: 31 X 95.

for both sides   winners & losers   so called so close
ly bound   as darkness leaves   bring tidings

of the fall   stumbling toward winter   its snow
hope for a blow (phffoooff)   erasure never to be dis/covered

angels in the snow   that indited absence
is my heart   youre marching across

in perfect formation   on the way to where
what   country of dreams   dreamt apart from geography

touch   stone   when blood is belief
a wooly thought   is brotherhood   *contra* . . .

so that what i breathe   'as darkness rises'   still
behind the men their arms outstretched in search

light   bright as black   (iff iff)   a half century
on   is the casual & stunning   'body-odour of race'

breath ghazal 71:

but whose   & who says those things
in a moment of deep despair & hatred

something broke the bounds   & many
massed   missed nuance   & applauded

but not all   it is   a place
i knew   the snows of yesteryear's

mountain   & the air i breathed then
fresh   too many here & there speak

with no shame   breathe ego   breathe
small   'my' country (land i love   still here

breath ghazal 72:

the angels have come again among us
they say   but angels

do they breathe   the sighs
or soughs their wings make might sound

like breathing   & its said they
spoke once   this tokens breath   air

taken in   yet   so much closer to perfection
they might never need to take breath

Ah ha we say   on the inhalation of
the sweet air surrounds them

which they do not breathe themselves
nor do they stay   or even care we may

breath ghazal 73:

hey   ya   a breath to sing a
song breathed out aah   oooh   &

baby   baby   ooh ooh ooh   oh i know
that   gone tune   long note held

& holding together the whole shebang
uh efff   oh fffaa   a blue   trusted

bent i mean to say   sung &
twisted note   affirming   all

the indrawn breaths reserves
of hope   of loss   of song singing out

breath ghazal 74:

i wonder how you breathe as you read me
face ive never seen lit by the glow of the screen

scrolling & sniffing out what secrets in the light
between the words   on a held intake

of breath efff   do you   suddenly
perceive connections I cant know   i make

with you   whose words release fffmm
affords me pleasure too   so we share

the air we breathe so   far apart   unknowing
that cloud dark   over there   fading winter exhalation

breath ghazal 75:

summers sun burns & shimmers now
thickens even city trees to a sensed impasto

bright colours   bright eyes   touch
'that all my desire goes

out'   into that glowing pastel
world unfurled in what gods lost breath

last breath cast upon the molten air
ah no   not stopping there   efff

desire   the inhalation continuing
on   something held fast there

in the body   'impossibly' turning
& reaching out to touch the 'beautiful'   beyond

how does the body know impossibly
awaits its perception   a sigh

s a sign desire sings it will
go out   towards   beyond   for

stars shine so small in the dark night sky
efff   fffmm   effff   aaah   more

& THE RETURNS

Excellence is walking through the open door
so choose an instrument you greatly love, and play.

Ocean.   Gull.   Home.
Lesbos is a long, wide way from here.

We could fill the distances ourselves
since Sappho has taken to her bed.

. . . .

She always does emerge. Let me tell you this, she'll say,
someone in some future time will think of us.

Dinah Hawken

Two Chinese tracings

i

would Tu Fu note
the single leaf a
float in the bird bath
behind the small &
indistinguished house down
that back lane

the moon *was*
high   & if you
stood in the right
place youd see it
cut in two   by
that leaf

no lights in
the windows of that house 'i'
shouldnt have
been there   nor
                         'you'

the water smelled
old   the moon
was new
               again

the leaf   now
simply floating
neither old   nor
new   like
you   as you step
into my poem
with Tu Fu

making arrangements

of stones   perhaps
or words
that 'leaf'
the way it   'floats'
'on'
the 'moon'
shining in the
'water'   in
the   'dark'

                ii

So we follow Li Po
into the garden

he leads us on
into the night
shadows   & light
of the moon   bright
            angel   riding our desires

glow in a glass
liquor of moon / shine of

gold coin in a bird bath
            path across a stream the trees
interrupt   we
interrupt his gentle
poems   pull us on
            beyond stream & trees
to a wide beach
            ocean   opening out to

56

the moon
s high way   Li Po
walks on   gentle
poet   pull us   on   in
to the water

                  it is warm   tastes

awful   wake
                  up

the dream of poetry
desired / drowned

The Al Purdy Dream Poem in the Athens Archeological Museum

another too long day in Athens & i'm unhappy
with the place   these people not the greeks i know
in books or on Kriti   not know but meet feeling
somehow safely at home   not at home
but feeling like that   not here   Athens
is out to get me   till we enter the relative
coolness of the archeological museum

wander among the statues & jewelry   the
armour of too many ancient wars   corpses
fed back to earth   their coverings only
to be dug up for this display
                                          & there in one room
some perfect marble physiques behind me
i find it
              on the wall   a single arm   the hand
gesticulating   finger lifted   (no   not that but)
as the man's rhetoric lifted the crowd

& so waking too early the next morning
as the men yell to assemble the market
just behind our 'quiet in the centre of town' hotel
i know that arm was for someone   yes
the al purdy dream poem announces
& yet you will have to do   you know
what such a long-lost arm would mean

& the al purdy dream poem begins to speak
of those centuries   lost   when the lost
arm gestured lonely deep in the earth
& now it's in the open air   (more or less)
but alone
                          not just the sculptor long dead
& unknown but the sculpture   that

orator   philosopher   whomever   hortative
before his audience   &
there it is   lonely through the eons
that arm so full of human desire

as the crowd rose & roared approval
the mans eyes bright with promise
& the artists too   promising
what immortality to that famous speech
we never heard
                        only the al purdy dream poem
wandering too the world looking
for such signs of a human past
broken as all things human are broken
by the earth which crushes stone or smooth
bone or marble
                        that arm spoke to me   or

the al purdy dream poem did

saying it is like that   it is
always like that
drinking cold Cretan wine in Aghia Galini
cold Canadian beer in Ameliasburg
& wondering about the dark   the arm
in the dark now
speaking so softly   I cant quite hear

so much is lost   & yet so much
is found
                    sometimes angrily awake
in a city you dislike & wont ever comprehend
too early in the hot morning
flies buzzing above you in the still dark room

in the dream Daphne

the walls were built of books   it seemed
an i reflects in panes the dayblood flowing deeper into dark below
what you told me   i forget   within that room so full of words
& my words too   you edit you   particular
knowledge   wisdom   my pencil shifts
in an agony of change you tell me what it is i should do
beneath the artificial lights now flattening the surfaces
of desks & manuscripts   i do not understand in that moment
between sleeping & waking   I think
i know you once again in   that your purpose
eyes open to the dark   is gone

for Fred

Everybodys drunk dance isnt
symptomatic syntagmatic   even
the slow gasp of a tenor sax notes
dancing wordwise to the world
losing 'l' & taking too long into
consideration that deep breath 'i' thought i heard 'you'
singing your song in the night
fogging up the freeway you move
to write rungs of a ladder only
letters later leave to imagine gone
going for 'it' all over again   or
was that signing

for Robin Blaser

Listen!   you said
& showed us how to do it   but

hearing   that harder lesson
is what the poems deeply tell   how
what has been writ & said
echoes through other typed corridors

of carefully crafted 'voices'
          (those angels   speak
                    only   to be
                                        heard

for Gwendolyn MacEwan   (1941 - 1987)

the blue eyes of Lawrence of Arabia
were the empty skies endlessly receding
over the sands   dry mouth endlessly repeating
      words   words   words

              or only the zero Arabian mathematicians discovered
      on clear & starfilled nights
            when the cupola of the sky bent so far upward
                    it turned inside out

      dunes of a desert your imagination walked
            looking for water   the few scattered palms
      those few words of power   now
             only a mirage ?

whose voice called out to you   in your darkness
      across what span of years   & gulfs of class & gender

it felt just like that goddamn motorcycle rushing the air
& you didnt even raise your eyes

as the black truck   blindsided you   again

for Tom Pow:

the gift of your poem Tom
       its a kind of map pal
              (& to track those lines across yr open hand

as we each drive to the edge
       landscape or language
              where the horizon rides the winds favours

we re together here   as you say
       saying the words we need
          to get there again
                       (inscribed
                 a hello trails across oceans

falls one white flake at a time
caught brilliance in the streetlamps glow high above

& look how the page takes shape there
       that single thistle   shining ideogram
          green imprint on the opening field

for L. N.

My friend moon
i pulled a leaf
from the tree
to see you

[pulled the water
closer too   a thief
spills it   the leaf
floats] better

for Marius Torres

The poems on the mirror
                              glow
no   they cannot
reflect the moment
Torres moved *through* his own images
to that other world
                              from which
translations only
                              silvered & incomplete
can arrive

History: Manhattan - Montréal - Berlin

They had sentenced him. Me also, to over twenty long years. But of what. Boredom is for others, trying not to notice change. In the broken system, shift from without within. But I'm not coming not now no I'm changing 'coming' around to a reward for them. The first cocktail we could take: a Manhattan. Drunk then and we could take anything. Berlin perhaps.

I'm through being guided. Poems are by the way. A song is signal enough, and in those days the stairway to heavens. You say I'm not only guided but it's by the text. This heretofore unacknowledged birthmark is language on parole. Remember: my razor cut skin. But now I'm a sucker guided through labyrinths by monks offering the revelation of beauty in and of itself. Let our politicians sell weapons. Let the first be last. We know that. Take off for Manhattan; sing loud then sing soft. We hear you take chances in Berlin.

I'd reread the novel. Really. Often, because I like it, a desire to learn how to live I guess. Something beside that? Well, theres you, that mystique, and baby, all the time I wondered. Talk about love; we talk about your version, how the body is part of and yet not it, your insistence on the spirit all dressed up and in there wearing your old and new clothes worn inside out. But someone might ask you if you can see something out beyond that horizon or coast line beyond its being there. You just keep moving across streets and through corridors down into the bowels of the station of the cross. I lost you but told them I saw you. Then much later I changed my story told someone else but you had disappeared so I went underground. Who told them that. Or you. But the photograph I took: that you was perfect and changed. One or one more of the records. Yeah, those.

You sang from the tower, loved all audiences equally, even me it seemed. It was as good a time as a song written for a loser could provide. Thats true but not fact and even now it matters more that youre putting body in music, worried about the changing voice that charted how you and I and everyone were aging just as predicted. It wasnt might alone would help you win. Whether weak or strong you sing deep and you know your casements open on the view of a forlorn way the tower throws shadows to the far horizon to stop the music. Lucky for me that didnt stop you. But when will democracy arrive. You preach or sing. I dont see the cracks I have to find. You found the way, but with what discipline. I want to know how, but the music, the many instruments combining, all these nights of joy. It's what I wanted, everything we ever prayed for; and even so this music isnt quite enough to change the world. We let it be again. Oh my, it will be hard work to shift the paradigm. Begin at the beginning, the first thing to do is we look for the light, take chances. Here or in Manhattan. I've been there too. Then becomes now there if we betray ourselves. This time take Luftansa's overnight flight to Berlin.

I passed through once by train, dont know anything first hand. You like it there I bet, and your audience loved you, youre in fashion always in Europe, it's less business than art, aint that right mister. Here they understand what the I in your songs is saying. Dont they. Yet what they really like is your romantic aura, all these signs of wild living, even drugs perhaps, experience anyway, a luck that we (I'm there too) cant keep ourselves from envying. Even when you meditate, spiritual, or loving, a thin man in black you sing. I listen in the dark and dont mind. There is something to like in your strange integrity, it's what keeps us listening, reading. It happened that like some I came to you through books. That was my way; it still is. My sister heard you singing on her first record. I dont know why we gave it to her. But take that for what it's worth. Manhattan has the best record stores. Then it did anyway. But now we can buy your music anywhere, take your music anywhere. Even to Berlin.

And if only the books traveled as I do, that easily. How we would thank transnationals if only they cared for you enough to care for literacy too. For they own the airwaves and all those other technologies; so books are superfluous items in the global marketplace, even yours that dig deeper into the crack that you have always sung about casually. I sent for each book; they all sent me elsewhere, looking for cracks and light. The indeterminacy principle at work: I couldnt monkey with the universe while standing apart and observing it. It always gets away. The cracks are everywhere, jagged lightning on plywood like Paterson Ewen's. I listen to violin or saxophone when I write and I suspect you have; while the painter practised listening to like sounds. I think every body dances to some music now. Night and day she stands before you and, amused and naked, waits for the now of eyes widening to the brightness. I'm here she says now are you ready. Down on your knees, thats the first gesture. Now look in the cracks. We have to do this together, lets take our time. You find them in Manhattan, in Montréal, even in that monastery. Then once more, over and over again we learn the first lesson: what to take with us, on our way to Berlin.

Remember, thats the key, you used to be me or somebody when you read or sang I understood you were talking to me. I used to believe in intimacy, something you gave to all of us, audience as I, to live in the light of song and changes. For better or worse, always the return of music, it changes it is the same. We remember performances, voices, and melodies to love. Oh, me? There are so many of us now. I and I once thought all your records brought something special to the ambient surround. Take your collage for Suzanne. I mean corsage. Arcane groceries float about our lady of

68

the harbour. In one sense they always have. I think it's necessary to remember that too. All our father's gifts, our mother's nurturing inspire you. That day you drove all night listening to music and loving your friend forever then wrote down everybody's tender teenage dream that I wont be wounded by time like the others youre the first one ever to know this thats what we read and heard. History teaches us to take the long view. By the waters of Manhattan you sat down and wept. To write then those Chelsea Hotel blues. No matter where we go, everywhere in the world, give or take a few small towns in Canada, is Berlin.

W[H]earing it
Fragmented memories

I know the song well & for me it always
had that end of December feeling,
a way of writing you now, singing the
good times as well as the bad. I also wore a
raincoat in New York's cold or anywhere I'm living.
Then there's music meant to last all thru the evening,
a slow orgasm of tears deep in the desert of song. I never could afford a
Burberry but he could, or did, the proceeds of some kind of record
I bought (& later the CD I'm listening to this moment), & you did too. I
got it – the joke, the book, the song's contrapuntal ironies
in those doubled words he didn't need to go to
London to learn. Now you, I, even he
in all his fame & glory, look so much older than in
1959.   Because we are.

It seems to be a way of slipping the self, that ego
hung out through the open window (flung out), ironically the
more he escaped the more he was trapped
heroically going to the station to meet every train
when not one would take him far enough away from
I.   Who changed his face so often,
took pains to hide, yet always came back
out from the monastery, the recording studio,
the little house on Hydra. In Paris,
lining the streets outside L'Olympia
and cheering for the 23rd encore, the beast
achieved critical mass and gave him the
glory he insisted he refused to seek.
When later that voice goes lower
the lines refuse the easy rhyme just for the
frayed moment: raincoat, Jane, you, & the

sleeves torn at the shoulder
were part of the guesswork, loss, forgiveness, all
repaired like the coat. The enemy sleeping now
with your woman (Jane?) may be
a taste of the trouble you took from her eyes, some
little lock of hair for remembrance, the black
leather coat that replaced that famous blue one finally.

Things tend downwards, hard days turn worse. Those
were the days, the nights, the voice more or less
clear. Enough for poetry and song.

I mostly listen to others now, those tough women, but
knew those lyrics well &
how the lyric lies in wait
to catch the imagination still,
dress it up
in identification, or at least overhearing
those sly come-ons we still believed in the
days before we took Berlin.

Turning back: a pastoral

for John Kinsella

That is a philosophical notion &
the only way to get there is via the
Theocritan backlanes of the mind. I drove a
ute (but we dont say that in Canada) my first time, or
has my memory as usual
been turned around. A youngster well-
versed in sexual fantasy I saw the event-horizon already

in the white bodies gleaming in a backlane
country night. Intent on
things beyond my experience it
seems I gazed down & imprinted the
obvious image on my brain forever as
the truck swept past & even the
velour of the seat back felt extreme.

On that night I thought for
the first time I knew what I had seen beyond the
dashboard light: those anonymous
crazy lovers were my teenage image of pastoral glory
with the moonlit passion I imagined
fresh as a film I might never see & all in plein
air. The nostalgic breeze is always

rushing past the open window
through which I had seen
the act my brother driving hadnt.
Doorless are the pathways to the
cabin we might come to in
the gentle night of the poem, where no ones
cursed & the wide blue shining

skies are always sunny although
blackened with clouds glimpsed suddenly
by flashes of lightning only at
night when rain should (& does) fall.
Though to get to those special places now youd have to adopt
a highway. You pay (not pave) your way to paradise where a
moon is always full & the stalker never
lurks in shadow to pounce. Is this not so?

Somewhere else it may be so
and we have to believe it: that
the green continues to grow even as the
spotlight of industrial colonization brightens,
cutting to the charred bone, trees going
through new contortions just to wave above the highways.

The sense of a common past's both lost & found in
burn-back as if the argument
of trees carried on across all
summer, & who then
detects a functional myth for tourism and bathing in
the blackened ash where even the sudden
jerks of light impressionism brings can speak only

of the desired realm (unfound). In the city somewhere
nerves are bad to-night
and a whole civilisation dies in a
tissue of lies on TV insistent that
the virtual pastoral is sufficient unto itself alone. Like
rabbits all voting for the same party we want to keep others
out of our intentional dreams,
to somehow turn the thin skin of civitas one colour again.
Chew on that & tell me

the world is safe from such predators. Somewhere even now
burnt flesh is the sacrifice that
prongs god awake again. For what. Is that the only tale
of the tribe we can tell. In the ashy
stubble such fire leaves we might discover
the remnants of salty dreams,
halogens broken harvest.

Conflagration burns away memory:
filling the mind with flame, scorching
the pastoral dream to degree zero. On
omni-screens everywhere the only fields

within sight are parking lots,
their harvest gets us where our
eyeballs point & nowhere does the gleam of
the green register as more than a
crack in the pavement. Between nature
and the tourists the
whine of hard drives crashing replaces the dream

of artists seeking to define
a way of life. It's a
triple palimpsest at least, way beyond the
two borders we once crossed awake & dreaming &
mocks any desire we might still feel for
its long lost
rituals of accommodation, acceptance,
a way of informing the mind, a
sign that the path still led to a forest spring

of love & immersion in the always
fading forest of innocence. Not
influence, not investment
in those open spaces of
a bargain, but we never knew that or we forgot. Beyond that
field is another, then another, & a wood
where to name the landscape so you can make it exist demands
gravity of purpose also lost. It

is therefore impossible for even
a citizen of such desire to avoid the bottle-
neck of enterprise, the final
chop of that final tree,
and get back to
the country in any
poem or song that
is not (on CD) already so
framed & so defined
by the torque of nostalgia.
Levity seems the only way out — but lacks grace.

Notes

Breath Ghazal # 9 is a homolinguistic translation (structural) of Leonard Cohen's 'The Asthmatic.'
Most of the poems in '& the returns' identify the writers they are for and from. Daphne is Daphne Marlatt; Fred is Fred Wah.
'History: Manhattan - Montréal – Berlin' and 'W[H]earing it./ Fragmented memories' are homolinguistic translations for Leonard Cohen, the first a structural one from a lyric sheet, the second a word/line acrostic from the notes to 'Famous Blue Raincoat'; 'Turning Back: A Pastoral' is a word/line acrostic based on John Kinsella's 'The Rabbiters: A Pastoral' from *The Hunt & other poems*.